Top Gs Like Me

Samson Hawkins

methuen | drama

LONDON • NEW YORK • OXFORD • NEW DELHI • SYDNEY

METHUEN DRAMA
Bloomsbury Publishing Plc, 50 Bedford Square, London, WC1B 3DP, UK
Bloomsbury Publishing Inc, 1359 Broadway, New York, NY 10018, USA
Bloomsbury Publishing Ireland, 29 Earlsfort Terrace, Dublin 2, D02 AY28, Ireland

First published in Great Britain 2026

Cover photography by Matt Crockett

Art direction and design by Rebecca Pitt

A catalogue record for this book is available from the British Library.

Library of Congress Control Number: 2026933030

ISBN: PB: 978-1-3506-4034-4
ePDF: 978-1-3506-4035-1
eBook: 978-1-3506-4036-8

Series: Modern Plays

Typeset by Mark Heslington Ltd, Scarborough, North Yorkshire

For product safety related questions contact productsafety@bloomsbury.com.

To find out more about our authors and books visit www.bloomsbury.com and sign up for our newsletters.

ROYAL & DERNGATE, NORTHAMPTON

Chief Executive **Jo Gordon**
Artistic Director **Jesse Jones**

Royal & Derngate is proud of its reputation as a thriving regional theatre, and was recently named the UK's Most Welcoming Theatre in the 2025 UK Theatre Awards. An important entertainment hub for all communities across Northamptonshire and beyond, the three-stage and cinema complex is home to an acclaimed *Made In Northampton* self-produced programme as well as welcoming some of the most well-known acts and shows touring the UK. In recent years the venue has celebrated Stage, Olivier and Academy Awards nominations, notably including a prestigious win for Best Family Show at the 2020 Oliviers. As important as the work on its stages, its nationally recognised Creative Engagement programme works with schools, families and communities, and the Generate development programme supports hundreds of regional artists each year, at all stages of their careers.

Highlights of 2025 included co-productions of a new *Made in Northampton* production of Hugh Whitemore's *Breaking the Code*, Dave Harris's *Tambo & Bones* in co-production with Actors Touring Company and Stratford East, and the Bruntwood Prize-shortlisted *(the) Woman* in association with New Perspectives, with *Mog's Christmas* rounding off the year. Other recent home-grown productions have included the world premiere stage adaptation of *Mog The Forgetful Cat*, the national and international tour of Agatha Christie's *And Then There Were None*, Spymonkey's *The Frogs*, Simple8's *Moby Dick*, a brand-new adaptation of *The Jolly Christmas Postman* and partnerships with Paines Plough on *My Mother's Funeral: The Show* and with the Rose Theatre in Kingston on Kazuo Ishiguro's adaptation of *Never Let Me Go*. In addition to *Top Gs Like Me*, productions for 2026 will include a new comedy *Party Season* created by The Wardrobe Ensemble and *What The Ladybird Heard at Christmas*.

Visiting productions on both the Derngate and Royal stages include musicals, dance, comedy and music, and its two-screen cinema presents the best in world, independent, British and mainstream film. Regularly hosting major civic events including graduation ceremonies, conferences and gala celebrations, it also provides a home for amateur theatre companies, school and youth performance groups, and choirs and community groups from across the county. Embedded in this programme is a regular schedule of access-enabled productions.

Box Office 01604 624811

www.royalandderngate.co.uk
Facebook: /royalandderngate
Instagram: @royalderngate
BlueSky @royalderngate.bsky.social

Royal & Derngate Team List

Chief Executive
Jo Gordon

Executive Assistant
Caroline Dalton-Bettles

ARTS TEAM

Artistic Director
Jesse Jones

Associate Director (Engagement & New Work)
Erica Martin

Schools & Young People Associate
Anna Simpson

Creative Engagement Assistant
Kyle Collingwood, Danielle Corr

FINANCE TEAM

Finance Director
David Gibson

Finance Manager
Laura Burton

Finance Officer
Sue Wilton

Finance Analyst
Ian Minney

Payroll Clerk
Stephanie Forde

PEOPLE AND CULTURE TEAM
Head of People & Culture
Dayna Preston

People Advisors
Simone Ellwood, Lemuel Ghann

People Assistant
Susan Ogunnaike

MARKETING, SALES & DEVELOPMENT TEAM
Director of Marketing, Sales & Development
Chris Evans

Head of Marketing & Digital
Chris Lowe

Communications & Content Manager
Amanda Howson

Senior Campaigns Officer
Georgina Haynes

Marketing Assistants
Rebecca Cockcroft, Rachel Thomas

Sales & Revenue Manager
Daniel Seath

Box Office Manager
Sophie Hinds

CRM Systems Manager
Christopher Wright

Sales, Data & Revenue Assistant
Thomas Kirby

Sales Supervisors
Helen Clifford, Amy Cutliffe, San-D Godoy-Messenger, Sophie Hinds, Sophia-Jay Sanderson, Nicola Stagg

Sales Advisors
Shannon Collyer, Jesse Cooke, Emily Granger, Ellen Hackett, Sophie Hinds, Gillian Lockwood, Louise Pinches, Sarah Potter, Katie Powell, Nicole Prestidge, Karen Sheen, Alina Wallace

Development Manager
Chris Smith

Development Assistant
Jo Scully (Maternity leave)
Sophia-Jay Sanderson (Maternity Cover)

PRODUCING & PROGRAMMING TEAM
Deputy CEO (Producing & Programming)
Holly Gladwell

Senior Producer
Remy Moynes

Senior Programmer
Zoe Albiston

Film Programme Officer
Rick Clifford

Producing & Programming Assistant
Laura Barton

Head of Production
Claire Hardacre

Head of Wardrobe
Victoria Youngson

Deputy Head of Wardrobe
Abbie Pillet

Head of Workshop
Sam Wilcox

Deputy Head of Workshop
Sam Fransch

Carpenter/Propmaker
Andrew Pike

Head of Scenic Art
Gina Hammersley (Maternity Leave)

Scenic Artist
Bronwen Herdman (Maternity Cover)

Props & Furniture Supervisor
Darren Abel

OPERATIONS & COMMERCIAL TEAM

Operations & Commercial Director
Rob Parkes

Operations & Commercial Coordinator
Oskar White

ICT Manager
Alan Stratton

CUSTOMER EXPERIENCE TEAM

Head of Customer Experience
Lorna Dawson

Customer Experience Managers
Rudi Gibbins, Hannah Denton, Leanna Harradine, Erica Mynard

Customer Experience Supervisors
Ryan Chambers, Liz Clancy, Curtis Dix, Rebecca Fisher, Amina Moss, James Swindall, Oskar White

Customer Experience Team Members
Emily Abraham, Mohammad Ahmed, Amelia Alderman, Isabella Aldridge, Topaz Alger, Tanya Allen, Georgia Anderson, Ellie Bilson, Charlotte Biseker, Aimee Blackburn, Samuel Boss, Leah Brown, Donovan Browne, Elliot Boor, Freya Browett, Imogen Burn, Robert Byford, Poppy Byrne, Grace Byworth, Jeanne

Carr, Brandan Childe, Liz Clancy, James Collins, Stevie Collins, Matthew Cook, Ez Cooke, Eve Collins, Benji Dotan, Sadie Douglas, Barbora Ejemova, Samantha Ellis, Nkem Emefiele, Owen Fantarrow, Georgia Farr, Charlie Franklin, James Franks, Alice Freed, Celine Freeman, Lisa Gidney, Josh Hamilton, Selin Hara, Owen Harradine, Hannah Heath, Dwight Hewitt, Luke Hobday, Samuel Hodder, Zoe Holloway, Maria Hopton, Phoebe Hutchinson, Joseph Kempster, Sandra Key, Claire Kiff, Jodie Kindell, Abi Kinder, George King, Sarah King, Erin Kinnear, Thomas Kirk, Ruth Knight, Sophie Lawlor, Antony Letts, Holly Lowe, Georgia Mackness, Jan Mackness, Ethan McInerney, Jenny McLoughlin, Millie Metcalfe, Mujahid Mohammed, Jessica Morris, Yuki Ohashi, Caitlin O'Kane, Alison Oliver-Harris, Ned O'Sullivan, Tracy O'Sullivan, Caitie Pardoe, Emilia Payne, Andrew Percival, Keira Perry, Amy Pike, Katie Powell, Lottie Powell, Zoe Quilter, Wendy Rawlings, Rimini Reed, Kiel Rennie, Olivia Roberts, Megan Rowles, Henry Rutter, Erin Searing, Harry Searing, Zarina Shah, Phoebe Smart, Carol Smith, Madeleine Spittles, Caitlin Stewart, James Swindall, Charlie Townsend, Lucy Watson, Samuel West, Eleanor Whitestone-Paul, Sally Whitestone, Olivia Whyatt-Sames, Jill Willis, Jane Wilson, Jana Wooll, Jessica Wright, Maddy Yoxall

MAINTENANCE TEAM

Maintenance Technician

Jonathan Cobb

General Maintenance Assistant

Daniel Bebber, Mary Jarvis Chisholm, Paul Curtis, Curtis Dix, Rebecca Fisher, Paul Gamble-Asten, Owen Harradine, Arthur Lewis, Ethan Monk, Daniel Morton

Format Change Crew

Darren Abel, Dhiren Basu, Daniel Bebber, Paul Browne, Martin Chisholm, Paul Curtis, Curtis Dix, Oliver Edwin, Rebecca Fisher, Louis Hackett, Lee Hopkins, Arthur Lewis, Damien Lord, Sarah-Jane Lord, Zoe McLean, Ethan Monk, Daniel Morton, Thomas Murray, Timothy Needham, Ryan Page, Dave

Reeve, Chloe Stevens, Jonathan Stewart, Christopher Waite, Oskar White, Andrew Withers, Neal Withers

TECHNICAL TEAM

Technical & Maintenance Manager
Steve Jarvis

Head of Stage (Derngate)
Daniel Morton

Deputy Head of Stage
James Chapman, Neal Withers

Head of Lighting & Sound (Royal)
Jo McIlwaine

Head of Lighting & Sound (Derngate)
Christopher Waite

Deputy Head of Lighting & Sound
Ethan Monk, Andrew Withers

Senior Technician (Lighting & Sound)
JB Pike, Fleur Tosney

Senior Technician (Stage)
Dhiren Basu, Louis Hackett, Christopher Rice

Technical & Maintenance Technician
Ryan Page

Technician (Cinema)
Clare Stannard-Clifford

Technician (Maintenance)
Lesley Thompson

Stage Door Receptionists
Ann Anderson, Jan Hall, Arthur Lewis, Sarah-Jane Lord, Fiona McLean, Zoe McLean

Technical and Production Crew
Amelia Alderman, Ann Anderson, Jessica Ball, Daniel Bebber, Adam Bee, Jonathan Blunsdon, Scott Bradley, Aaron

Brotherhood, Mason Button, Lewis Byfield, Luke Cannon, Martin Chisholm, Jacob Clark, Helen Clifford, Antony Coles, Ethan Corbidge, Jacob Corbidge, Freya Cox, Adam Oscar Darby, James Delamere, Jude Devoil, Katie Di Stefano, Curtis Dix, Bethany Dover, Matt Duffy, Nick Freeman, Nikola Golding, Josh Green, Rob Griffiths, Ashleigh Hammond, Claire Hardacre, Edward Holiday, Aiken Holland, Cat James, Joseph Jeffery, Poppy Kensett, Stephanie Kensett, Robert Kidd, James King, Victoria King, Arthur Lewis, Sarah-Jane Lord, Fiona Luck, Joanne Marshall, Andy McGrath, Daniel McGrath, Fiona McLean, Zoe McLean, Lewis McLean, Samantha McNern, David Middleton, Adam Monk, Ethan Monk, Rachel Monk, Tom Newell, Phoebe O'Reilly, Chris Paine, Tamsyn Payne, Aaron Pemberton, Alfie Pendred, Andy Pike, Gilles Pink, Sam Poulton, Ashley Radley, Jake Ralph, Dom Read-Jones, Christopher Rice, Connar Richards, Stuart Rogers, Charlie Rooney, Ellie Sanders, James Scotney, Amy Mae Smith, James Smith, Thomas Smith, Chloe Stevens, Jonathan Stewart, Vicky Stothard, Robin Tedds, Fleur Tosney, Ciaran Tunmer, Gemma Walton, Connie Watson, Oskar White, Sam Wilcox, Jimmy Wilkins, Dominic Young

ACCESS SERVICE PROVIDERS

Audio Describer
Caroline Burn

Audio Brochure
Calvert Creative Concepts

BSL Interpreters
Emma Phillips, Krista Norris, Donna Ruane, Maria Fellows

Captioning
Royal & Derngate

Access Advisors
Deaf Connect, Audio Description Association,
Northamptonshire Association for the Blind

Volunteers

Judy Adams
Linda Ashton
Lynn Babb
Ayla Bailey
Sarah Ball
Steve Ball
Rob Bartley
Mick Beeby
Karen Beirne
Glenys Billingham
Michelle Blunden
Brenda Bowers
Pauline Braithwaite
Anne Brook
Karen Brown
Sue Buckle
Helen Bull
Mike Burgess
Sally Carter
Jane Causebrook
Cary Cheney
Caroline Clancy
Hayley Clarke
Pam Cleavely
Millie Cleaver
Franki Cockayne
Martyn Cook
Rosemary Cook
Josh Cox-White
Tony Croft
Helen Da Costa Cooper
Julie Dale
Sandy Deacon
Julia Denton
Kayleigh Devlin
Peter Donabie
Rachel Donohoe
Linda Dunleavy
Jenny Eldred
Joanne Ellison
Brenda Galvin
Sally Goadsby
Una Gutteridge
Oliver Hague
Selin Hara
Lynne Hill
Mandy Howes
Lamaara Hughes-Watson
Jenny James
Evelyn Jarvis
Tony Jewson
Sue Jeyes
Robert Jones
Vivienne Jones
Avril Judge
Kieran King
Jean Kirk
Elizabeth Littlejohn
Barbara Marsh
Jane Marshall
Caroline Matthews-Maynard
Adrian McDowall
Jayne Miller
Helen Millett
Myra Munroe
Jenny Newnham
Lynne O'Sullivan
Bismah Parveen
Rihanna Patel
Celine Perkins
Theresa Rafferty
Michelle Reeve
Enid Rippon
Lee Robertson

Lily Rouse
Edward Ryan
Judith Sadd
Zarina Shah
Mo Shapiro
Vicky Smith
John Stevens
Julie Stobart
Lynn Stokes
Jennie Todd-Gordon
Sharon Toyer
Lesley Turner
Ken Underwood
Seema Verma
Doe Ward
Vanessa Watson
Brenda Weston
Giles Willson
Jean Wimpress
Sheila Woodhead
Ann Wright

Top Gs Like Me was developed with the support of the National Theatre's Generate programme.

Initially developed through the Royal & Derngate Generate programme in partnership with Andy Routledge.

Royal & Derngate Northampton's Made in Northampton season is sponsored by Michael Jones Jeweller.

SAMSON HAWKINS

WRITER

Samson is a playwright and screenwriter from Northamptonshire. Samson's debut full length play *Village Idiot* premiered at The Nottingham playhouse before playing the Ipswich New Wolsey and Theatre Royal Stratford East. Samson has recently adapted *Village Idiot* for television, to be part of Channel 5's revival of the iconic series *Play for Today* series.

Samson has previously written one act and short plays which have been performed at Soho Theatre, Leicester Curve Theatre, Nottingham Playhouse and The Edinburgh Fringe.

Samson is currently working on an adaptation of *The Reluctant Dragon* for the Marlowe Theatre to be performed Christmas 2026.

Samson has previously been a Resident Director of the Oxford Playhouse, an Associate Artist of the Leicester Curve & a New Perspective New Associate. He has also been part of the Royal Court Writers Group, Oxford Playhouse Playmaker & Soho Young Writers. Samson trained as an actor at East 15 and Italia Conti and as a theatre director at the Orange Tree Theatre. Samson is also a qualified secondary school teacher, currently working at a comprehensive school.

Top Gs Like Me was first produced by Royal & Derngate, Northampton, on 23 February 2026. The original cast and creative team were:

Cast

Mia	Fanta Barrie
Grace	Emily Coates
Hugo Bang	Danny Hatchard
Aidan	Daniel Rainford
Charlie	Finn Samuels
Dave	David Schaal

Internet Ensemble

Chris Adekanle, Hayley Adele, Ben Bayes, Aimee Bidwell, Lola Blackler, Brooke Bonney, Luke Collins, Harry Day, Abigail Field, Sabrina Gricolat, Selin Hara, Larna Hope, Sadie Hylott, Kane Simon Hunter, Robyn Khasan, Benjamin Lawley, Billy Mason, Kimberley Nakai Mandizha, Poppy Puttock, Louise Rae, Kit Robson, Amelia Ryan, Annabel Sherring, Liv Waters, Michael Wilde

Creative Team

Writer	Samson Hawkins
Director	Jesse Jones
Set & Costume Designer	Rebecca Brower
Lighting Designer	Rory Beaton
Sound Designer	Benjamin Grant
Movement Director	Monica Nicolaides
Fight Director	Kiel O'Shea
Dramaturg	Lauren Mooney
Casting Director	Kristian Wall
Voice & Dialect Coach	Gemma Boaden
Associate Director	Kitty Benford
Assistant Director	Amelia Michaels
Additional Dramaturgical Support	Andy Routledge

Scooter Coaching	Aiden McCrystal & Jayden Sharman

Please note the following material contains strong language and references to statutory rape.

Top Gs Like Me

IRL characters

Aidan, *18, gets distracted*
Mia, *18, a pleasure to have in class*
Charlie, *18, shows great leadership on the rugby pitch*
Grace, *14, it's just a phase*
Dave, *40-ish, who?*

Online characters

Hugo Bang
Hype Beast
Viral Accountant
Female Aquarius
Martin Luther King
Queen Elizabeth the Second
Donald Trump
Benjamin Netanyahu
Yoga Business Muscle Man
Rizz Man
Scooter Rider One
Scooter Rider Two
Boy in Car
Girl by Car
Street Interviewer
Angry Woman
Shop Assistant
Man in Suit
Military Man
Street Interviewee One
Street Interviewee Two
Phone Man
Muscle Man
Game Reviewer
Nerdy Man
American Woman
Spicy Swine
Man in One of Those Horrible American Suits
Theo Grossman

Poet
Princess from Japanese Video Game
Hero from Japanese Video Game
Two Bokoblins
Dancers

Setting

Radlands Plaza Skatepark, Bedford Road, Northampton, NN1 5PE.

Radlands Plaza. It's full of ledges, rails, pads, sliders, kickers, hips and many kinds of banks. It's council run, free to use and generally considered to be one of the top skateparks in the country. The skatepark is in the middle of a large park, one side of the park is Northampton University, the other is a retail park. It's not really in an area of Northampton, it's close to the villages which are essentially now part of the town, it's also walking distance to the town centre.

The thing about Radlands is that it's good, it's in Northampton, and it is good.

Also 'the internet', or more accurately TikTok, Reels, YouTube and Shorts. This is a post-algorithm internet, a personalised, curated internet. The internet of a young man from Northampton. It is also an increasingly AI infiltrated social media.

Scene One

Aidan *is wearing a Mortimer's staff top, baggy jeans, a beanie and some old Vans that are held together with a bit of gaffer tape.* **Aidan** *scoots around the skatepark with a sense of freedom. He tries a trick. He fails. He tries again. He fails again. He takes a moment, he adjusts his jeans, he breaths in. He tries the trick. He fails.*

He throws his scooter across the skatepark and storms off towards his bag. He gets out a pack of Yum Yums, peanut butter and jam. With skill, intensity and artistry, he uses his key to cut open the Yum Yums, he then uses his debit card to spread the peanut butter, and spread the jam. He takes a bite, it's heaven.

After the first bite, he gets his phone out, he starts to watch a video.

We enter internet land. While in internet land we can still see everything in the normal world, but we also have internet land. Internet land should be aggressively entertaining.

Two scooter riders come on stage.

Scooter Rider One Hello hello hello, we are here at All In Skatepark in Reading, tell 'em, Darren, what's about to go down?

Scooter Rider Two (*name of trick* **Aidan** *just tried*) Boy.

Scooter Rider One (*name of trick* **Aidan** *just tried*) Boy!

Both scooter riders do a (*name of trick* **Aidan** *just tried*).

Repeat.

Scooter Rider One Hello hello hello, we are here at All In Skatepark in Reading, tell 'em, Darren, what's about to go down?

Scooter Rider Two (*name of trick* **Aidan** *just tried*) Boy.

Scooter Rider One (*name of trick* **Aidan** *just tried*) Boy!

Both scooter riders do a (*name of trick* **Aidan** *just tried*).

A group of around five young women perform a dance – six seconds – skip.

A new group of more attractive women perform the same dance – fifteen seconds – skip.

A group of three men perform the same dance – two seconds – skip.

A young American man **Hype Beast** *wearing a Supreme cap, an Anti Social Social Club jacket, Burberry shorts and Yeezy trainers.*

Hype Beast Yo, what's up my guys, you're here for another awesome prank video where today, I'm going to dress up as a burglar, forcibly enter my nan's retirement home and threaten the residents with my Glock, forcing them to hand over them bank deets. Bang Bang Gran Gran!

A young woman dressed as the princess from a Japanese video game defeats two Bokoblins in slow motion to orchestral music – twelve seconds.

Hugo Bang *enters with a sword.*

Hugo Bang Barack Obama didn't kill Bin Laden, I did. Nine-eleven wouldn't have worked on me anyway, I wouldn't be one of the lemmings inside, oh no I'm scared of planes crashing into me. I'd see those jets coming, go King Kong on top of the tower, clothes line the first plane, tombstone pile driver the second, drop kick over the octagon. Time for breakfast.

A viral accountant and a female Aquarius enter.

Viral Accountant You have $20,000 of credit card debt, $75,000 of student debt.

$40,000 of car debt, $60,000 of medical debt, you owe your parents $15,000 and you don't have a job. What are you going to do?

Female Aquarius Well I'm an Aquarius so –

Skip.

The original group of around five young women now dressed in more typical skater clothing do the same dance – repeat three times.

Hugo Bang *enters.*

Hugo Bang Hello, Hola, Guten Tag, Je m'appelle. I can conjugate what you ponder, why has he acquired a sword? Wrong question. Incorrect inquiry. Why haven't you got a sword, pussy? Mine's got diamonds on the handle, and what. I travel back in time, 'Hey Pharoa Mufasa look at this', then, shiny shiny, he's distracted, cut out his heart, drink the blood, now I'm Moctezuma of Rome.

You got two choices, uno, do what they tell you, watch Netflix, watch Disney, eat the bugs, don't have a sword. Tres, shiny shiny stabby stabby swordy swordy. Don't be a moron. Wotcha.

A young women dressed as the hero from a Japanese video game wearing something similar to Majora's Mask, with two women dressed similarly to Bokoblins do the same dance to a drum and bass version of the Breath of the Wild Guardian theme.

It repeats until **Aidan***'s next line.*

Mia *enters, she wears a Carhartt fleece, light blue flared jeans and white Nike Air Maxes.*

Mia You going to show me it then?

Aidan Thought you'd never ask.

He goes to take down his trousers.

Mia The trick, you div.

Aidan Not sure you'd be able to see it from back there anyway. Need a telescope. Nah, I'm not doing the trick.

Aidan *starts to scoot around the space.* **Mia** *follows* **Aidan***'s lead. Throughout the scene they use the skatepark. The movement of the skating should follow the flow of the scene.*

Mia Why not?

Aidan Well the thing is, I physically, emotionally, spiritually, mess it up every time.

Mia It's the only reason I bothered coming down.

Aidan Cheers. And see cus like, you know how you're always saying I should believe in myself?

Mia You should.

Aidan You're wrong, I shouldn't. Useless advice. Worse than useless because it causes more failure. I can't do it. Never could, never will. Abject failure. Consistent catastrophe every time.

Mia Brilliant.

Aidan I reckon believe in yourself needs to have some, what d'you call it, caveats attached, you know what I mean? Because if you're someone who's like me, like, in general, a bit rubbish, the motto should be, 'Believe in yourself . . . within reason'.

Mia If you can't do the trick at least give me one of your things?

Aidan What are they called?

Mia Don't make me say it.

Aidan Respect the artistry.

Mia A Yum Yum Peanut Butter Jam Jam Glory.

Aidan Deluxe. They're called Yum Yum Peanut Butter Jam Jam Glory Deluxes now. I added the deluxe to make it sound more deluxe.

Mia Fantastic, can I have one then?

Aidan Dunno if you can afford it, they're pretty deluxe.

Mia Mates' rates?

Aidan You'd have to be my mate for that.

Mia Wow Aidan, you're so witty, has anyone told you how funny you are?

Aidan Yeah, your mum did last night.

Mia Did you show her your tiny balls?

Aidan No, just my arsehole, your mum is really into rimming.

Mia Incredible.

Aidan I think that's why you're a child of divorce, because your dad didn't like getting rimmed. Made him feel unmanly. Toxic masculinity, that is.

Mia Is that why your parents broke up as well?

Aidan No, my mum doesn't like rimming, that's rank. It's just specifically your mum who is really dedicated to the nuanced finesse of her signature rim job.

Mia Deep.

Aidan Like your mum's tongue.

Mia *stops scooting.*

Mia Can you stop?

Aidan You started it with my tiny balls, I don't start fights I finish 'em. Wotcha.

Mia You don't know where the line is.

Aidan Ah well, ADHD, all part of it, you ent allowed to criticise me, because if you do that'll be a hate crime.

Mia I'm not sure /

Aidan / Nah, you'll go prison. I got my certificate and everything. Only test I ever passed.

Mia Do you have a change of clothes?

Aidan Why, we going robbing?

Mia No, loads of my friends are going The Lab because it was the last exam today, well unless you do German, but I don't trust people who do German, so.

Aidan Is posh school still going? We finished at college ages ago.

Mia The boys' school isn't posh, it's just a selective sixth form.

Aidan That's worse.

Mia How?

Aidan *stops scooting.*

Aidan At least like, poor people can make some money and then send their kids to private school. Ent nothing you can do if you're genetically a bit thick though, is there? Condemned.

Mia How were we condemned at school if I made it out?

Aidan Because you ent genetically thick. And anyway, your mum would like read books, and take you places, and talk to you and that.

Mia Yea, basically Supernanny is Daphne.

Aidan And made sure you did your homework so you didn't get stuck with degenerates like me.

Mia It wasn't you that she wanted me away from, you were retro naughty, she wanted me out of the line of sight from the corridor kids.

Aidan Those corridor kids are our people.

Mia They're social services' people now.

Aidan Alright, big shot.

Mia If it wasn't for like, Rocco, Max, Cameron, Mo and Courtney it would have been alright, they just ruined it for everyone else.

Aidan We lost Rocco.

Mia He died? When?

Aidan No, him and his gran moved Aylesbury.

Aidan *skates off.*

Mia You coming to The Lab then?

Aidan You know my mum used to go there when it was the Labour Club.

Mia Yea, it's great, so you should get changed and come.

Aidan I can't wear my work uniform at the Labour Club?

Mia It's not an actual Labour Club anymore, for people with jobs, that's weird, it's fun now, they have a reggae night.

Aidan Ah jammin', nah I'll give it a miss thanks.

Mia You never go out.

Aidan *stops scooting in disgust.*

Aidan I went to Home Bargains yesterday!

Mia How many times do I have to tell you, Home Bargains isn't out!

Aidan It's not in! You can't say I'm staying in and then go Home Bargains. That's a lie, so it's going out.

Mia Do you ever get déjà vu?

Aidan Nah, just dyslexia.

Mia I can't have this conversation again.

Mia *starts to walk off.*

Aidan Why are you throwing a strop? I thought you came to watch me do the trick.

Mia Well you can't do it, can you?

Aidan Technicality, semantics . . . nit picker.

Mia If you want to come, then come, if you don't, then don't.

Mia *starts to walk off again.*

Aidan Your friends will be there though, won't they?

Mia Yea, that's the point, Aidan, that's why it's fun.

Aidan Not for me.

Mia Why not?

Aidan They just, last time, they kept asking me where the pesto was.

Mia Well, you were in your uniform, it was a funny joke.

Aidan It's annoying. It's like, you know, it's a, they're lemmings, it's a not funny joke.

Mia Where is the pesto, though?

Aidan It's not funny, Mia.

Mia But seriously though, red pepper pesto, do you? Don't give it out if you can't take it. It's not their fault you never change out of your uniform.

Aidan Because I had work, I actually have to have a job.

Mia I've got a job as well, you don't see me going to the pub repping Costa. I know it's not been like, good, but you can't just hang around Radlands by yourself and think it's going to get better. You spend hours going on about my mum licking your arsehole and then you get offended if someone mentions pasta sauces.

Aidan Alright, how about this. If I land (*Name of trick.*) then we stay here, but, if I don't, then we'll go.

Mia I'm going either way but sure.

Aidan Okay, I'll believe in myself.

Mia Very good.

Aidan *starts doing a little spiritual dance.*

Aidan (*from the song, 'Hooked on a Feeling' by Björn Skifs and the Blue Swede*) Ooooga chaka ooga ooga, ooga chaka.

Mia What are you doing?

Aidan I'm believing in myself. Getting in a positive mental attitude.

Mia I think that's offensive but I'm not sure who to.

Aidan Oooga chaka.

Aidan *tries to do the trick but fails.*

Bollocks.

Mia Great, so we going then?

Aidan Ah, but, I have a can of Monster in my bag with your name on it. I mean, it's actually Boost Energy and I want it but you can have my backwash.

Mia Charlie just messaged me, he's going to pick us up around the corner.

Aidan Who's Charlie?

Mia He's erm, he's my new, kinda, I'm, seeing him I guess?

Beat.

Aidan Oh like, oh, I didn't know, cool, cool cool cool.

Mia It's not like a big deal, as long as I get the results I'm going to Bristol in like two months, so, just a summer fun fling thing.

Aidan Ah, flinging wicked more like, sorry, good for you, good for Charlie, good for you and Charlie.

Mia Yeah.

Beat.

Aidan What and he has a car, does he?

Mia Yea, so he can pick us up.

Aidan Nah I'm good, I, I don't like getting picked up do I.

Mia He could probably do it. He's quite strong.

Beat.

That was a joke.

Aidan I'm sure he is. Good for Charlie, being strong, important. Strength. Strong man Charlie. Ring to it.

Beat.

Mia Are you, seeing anyone?

Aidan Yea someone from work.

Mia Oh really that's amazing, who is she?

Aidan Ruth on the fish counter, she's sixty-four but she can take a pounding like a champ.

Mia I think you could do better.

Aidan Hey, don't you go slagging off my imaginary GILF. She's all I got.

Mia You could probably get a really hot imaginary girlfriend. Believe in yourself.

Aidan Within reason.

Mia*'s phone goes.*

Mia Charlie's here so, if you're coming.

Aidan He drives quickly, don't he? Safe to get in a car with him? I'm not, I've er, Ruth wants me back so I can teach her to stream Midsummer Murders.

Mia You sure?

Aidan Yea, she loves John Nettles that one, obviously got a type.

Mia Okay well, maybe I'll bring Charlie here next Saturday?

Aidan Ah brilliant, yea great, would love to meet him, yea, what a guy, you two go have fun, you crazy kids.

Mia See you then.

Mia *exits.*

Aidan Good for Charlie.

Aidan *dissolves.*

Aidan (*to self*) Wish I had a sword then I could stab myself.

Aidan *tries the trick, fails.*

Do the trick, or break your neck and die, there is no other option.

Aidan *tries the trick but doesn't break his neck.*

Coward.

Aidan *gets out his phone, woohoo we are back in internet land, argh it's well bright.*

Martin Luther King *walks on stage.*

Martin Luther King I have a dream, that one day, I will be WWE Champion.

Martin Luther King *starts celebrating.*

A girl walks on stage. A boy driving a Ferrari drives on stage.

Girl by Car Oh my god, is that a Ferrari, how old are you?

Boy in Car Nineteen!

Girl by Car Nineteen! What do you do?

Boy in Car Drive a Ferrari.

A girl walks on stage. A boy driving a Ferrari drives on stage.

Girl by Car Oh my god, is that a Ferrari, how old are you?

Boy in Car Nineteen!

Skip.

A young man dressed in a tight t-shirt, wearing sunglasses and posing in an aggressively sexual way.

Rizz Man (*while biting his lip*) Oh hey girl, I didn't see you there, no, no I'm not trying to rizz you up, I'm just trying to, get to know you.

Skip.

Two boys fight each other while people scream.

Poet Society.

They bow.

Skip.

Queen Elizabeth the Second *comes on stage holding a microphone.*

Queen Elizabeth (*rapping*) I scored Diana, I'd do it again.
Sket in the four door mashed up, sipping champagne

A man holding an iPhone and wearing a backpack walks up to two women. The man films the women aggressively.

Street Interviewer Will you go out with me?!

Street Interviewee One Erm sorry, no I er, have a boyfriend.

Street Interviewer What about you then?

Street Interviewee Two No thank you.

Street Interviewer Ergh yet again fellas, more unarguable scientific evidence they won't tell you, females are shallow. Join the 'Men who absolutely could get girlfriends if they wanted to but are just choosing not to' Discord today.

Skip.

A man in suit jogs on stage.

Man in Suit Hi, oh sorry, you just caught me after getting back from my morning run. And I know what you are all thinking, how did I afford that house? Am I a lawyer, am I a doctor? No, I upload AI-read text onto Audible, and make millions.

A man in a military uniform enters the stage.

Military Man So, you can fight with your brother, then you can fight on the street. And if you can fight on the street, you can fight in the ring. And if you can fight in the ring, then you could learn to commit war crimes against Syrian toddlers on their way to nursery. So just join already, you got nothing else on.

Hugo Bang *enters, he chews on chewing tobacco and drinks Cactus Jack's Raspberry.*

Hugo Bang I'm perusing the multitude of DMs from females I get daily, and I scout this twilight's prey. Chantelle. Oh, she's continental, transcendental, probably mental. I mean, she is a woman after all. Ha ha, men are funny.

Returning to the Odyssey. Who are you, Chantelle, what do you long for? She requests food, I'll grant you something to consume. No pizza for my females, my females get meat.

I pull up in one of my seventeen Lotus Elises. And what do I identify? Big, white, posh – not her, the house. She's hung curtains, for which I deduce she's classy and intelligent, not my usual type. The curtains appear white, which means she's either a clean freak or she knows how to lurk in the shadows. What are you hiding from, Chantelle, do you need protection?

She has foliage on the vicinity of her property, environmentalist, loves orangutans probably. She longs to save the world but is fearful she's just a sardine in a sea full of killer whales. She needs a walrus to help her to the beach. (*Makes walrus noises.*) I am the walrus, goo goo g'joob.

I ring the door bell, steak in one hand, keys to one of my twenty-nine Lotus Elises in one hand, and my dick in the other. Breath goes in, breath goes out, it's like a metaphor.

Beat.

Idioms.

Grandly, she zips the door open. She's wrapped in a towel, and just a towel. 'Oh hello there, I'm sorry I'm not dressed', she hypothesises. She's untruthing of course, she deliberately got undressed and then re-dressed in a towel when she saw I was here, I can tell because I know females. She is trying to weave her web of lies, it's okay, Chantelle, I'll wriggle into your trap, you eight-legged freak.

Here's my opportunity, I put down the keys to one of my forty-seven Lotus Elises and show her my eToro account and my growing property portfolio of student lets in Derby. She's Niagara Falls but I keep going, I lean on the wall in my own patented way, which lets her know I am an alpha man who does not follow the crowd in the way that he leans. She asks for financial advice, and I tell her, the only financial advice females need is to stick with Hugo Bang. And that's why, comrades of currency, it's make cash, smash gash, in that order.

Hugo Bang *exits.*

Two girls dressed as the princess and the hero from a Japanese video game come on stage and do a TikTok dance. **Hugo Bang** *enters.*

Hugo Bang Oh yea, and then we had sex, if you know what I mean.

A chorus of people applauds **Hugo Bang**.

Scene Two

The next morning, **Aidan** *sits on a ledge using his phone.* **Aidan** *puts down his phone, gets out his scooter and tries the trick, he fails.*

Dave, *a man considerably older then the rest of the characters, enters holding a can of San Miguel. He wears old trainers with jogging bottoms tucked into socks, a large unironed checked shirt, a tweed jacket and possibly a statement hat. He speaks with an affected upper-class accent.*

Dave Good morning, old chap.

Aidan No it's not.

Dave Oh excuse me, I must have been mistaken.

Aidan Mia has a boyfriend.

Dave Good for Mia.

Aidan No, not good for Mia, bad for Aidan. He's got a car. Last night I had this nightmare of a Fiat Punto shagging my mum at Mortimer's.

Dave Everyone has a car.

Aidan I don't.

Dave You've got something grander, a what do ya call it, scooter. That nifty little gadget is quite the thing.

Aidan Yea, I'll give her a backy, that'll rizz her up. How am I meant to compete with him? He goes to her school, so he's smart. He's got a car, so he's rich. He's apparently stronger than Hercules. Mia's got John Cena laying the SmackDown on her every Sunday morning while I'm at the skatepark with some depressing alchy who lives in a shit caravan by the big roundabout.

Beat.

No offence.

Dave I'll have you know, the council repossessed my caravan so I'm back to Tentington Manor.

Aidan Ah shit mate, my mum's already on the sofa at ours like, but maybe you /

Dave / Don't you worry about me, boy, I've had my day, you need to concentrate on yourself. You're young.

Aidan I'm screwed.

Dave You've boundless potential, the world is your oyster.

Aidan Nah it's not, I ent ever even had an oyster, world's only your oyster if you can afford oysters.

Dave You've got two jobs, you're a career-focused individual.

Aidan Yea, Mortimer's and DeliverEats, sixteen hours a week and what, Elon Musk better watch out.

Dave You just need to keep your head down, and I'm sure the bosses at DeliverEats will admire your gusto and you can work your way up the ladder.

Aidan I'm not taking career advice from a man who lives in a tent. It's not the nineties anymore, you can't do well from like, working in a job. You've got to own things. Get with the times, El Davo.

Dave Yes well, that may be true, however, living with your mother then you must be saving /

Aidan / Mum's sick, en it.

Dave Again?

Aidan Still.

Dave Oh.

Aidan Yea.

Dave That's not ideal.

Aidan What do you mean? I thought all the birds wanted to see a bloke between his takeaway deliveries and then go back to his flat where his mum just lays on the sofa staring into the abyss.

Dave I've had worse offers.

Aidan I need to like, better myself, en it.

Dave You need to be the real you.

Aidan Nah, real me's rubbish.

Dave You should focus on knuckling down, working hard, you will get there, my boy.

Aidan Nah El Davo, that's what they want us to believe.

Dave Who are they?

Aidan You know, they, them lot, over there, doing the stuff. Telling us to eat slugs and watch Pocahontas.

Dave Pardon?

Aidan You know, eat slugs. Bugs! And watch, doesn't matter, what matters is I need to be like, be the best me. Because, like, average Charlie, that's the Ultimate Warrior who Mia's with, is better than average Aidan. But if I'm working on like hundred per cent brain power, looks maxing, style maxing, maybe need to sort my jaw out, like mew and that, mouth tape, gym maxing, sit ups, and then like, I'm already well funny.

Dave Do girls find you funny?

Aidan Yea like, reckon so, probably, maybe, when I tell jokes Mia does tell me to stop quite a lot. But that's like, women do that though, don't they? Nah, she finds me funny. Ah no.

Dave What?

Aidan I bet he's tall.

Dave He's most likely taller than you.

Aidan I'm like, average, ish, lower side of average. World wide I'm taller than average actually, like, I'm a big man, globally, from the international perspective I'm a very large male. And Mia's well left wing, so she loves like, the world and that. Yea like, she's a communist, so she can't discriminate against small men, so that's fine. Was Stalin small? Yea, Stalin was small and I bet he got it.

Dave And that's who you wish to emulate to gain the love of Mia, Comrade Joseph Stalin.

Aidan Yea, reckon so. And I've always been like, bold. School report always said I was a disruptive influence, it takes a big presence to be a disruptive influence. Big man Stalin, that's me.

Dave Well, if you were like Stalin, you'd lend me ten pounds.

Aidan You serious?

Dave You know I find it ever so embarrassing to ask.

Aidan I hate being asked more than you hate asking.

Dave You don't.

Aidan I do, every time you ask I get £10 poorer and you get £10 richer.

Aidan *looks in his wallet.*

Aidan Well you, you'll get (*While counting coins.*) £4.27 richer.

Dave You don't have any more?

Aidan Jesus Christ man, do you want my shoes as well? I can shave my head and try see what we get for the hair. Sell my kidney? How am I ever going to make money?

Dave What do other people do to make money? Who owns DeliverEats or Mortimer's? You should emulate them, not Stalin, and by the time you get to my age . . .

Aidan I'll be Sir John DeliverEats. I had an idea for my course but my teacher said it was dumb.

Dave Surely anyone who understood business wouldn't be teaching it, they'd be doing it.

Aidan Yea, I thought it was good, cus, right, you know how like, if you order from DeliverEats, you buy a curry.

Dave I am aware of the concept, yes.

Aidan Yea but, people also get like, drinks, cans, and then like, Ben and Jerry's. But it's well expensive. So people are like £8 Ben and Jerry's, fuck that, £2.50 can of Diet Coke, nah mate.

Dave So there is no gap in the market.

Aidan Oh there is, Daverooney, there is if there was a driver, or lots of drivers, who could offer them the products they just turned down, for less money, right at their door.

Dave If you sell the product at a loss, then you will lose money.

Aidan I get fifteen per cent off at Mortimer's. Staff discount. Using the system to fight the system.

Dave A snake eating its own tail.

Aidan Reach around.

Dave In theory, it could be possible.

Aidan Issue is, see, Sir John DeliverEats got all us little minions doing all the actual work for him, and he just hoovers up all the money, I can't do that, because who could I get that's below me to take advantage of?

Beat.

The homeless!

Dave Aidan.

Aidan It's not like you lot got a lot on!

Dave You don't understand the nuanced practicalities of life on the peripheries of society.

Aidan Alright, Legend of El Davo, you're hardly going round completing quests for rupees, you just ask teenagers for San Miguel money.

Dave It's a lovely idea, but it isn't something I could be involved with.

Aidan Nah, you gotta believe in yourself, DaveMania, because this summer, this is our last chance. This is my last chance to get what I want. And you, you're signing up for DeliverEats, you're delivering some stuff, and you're selling some cans on the side.

Without you I'm just running a tuck shop in the school toilets, but with you, it's a business, it's a corporation. You joining turns me from a twat into a CEO.

Dave Start without me and /

Aidan / We are starting today. We need to.

Dave These things take planning, patience.

Aidan She's leaving in two months. She's going to Bristol in two months' time. In three months' time she'll have dreadlocks, in four months she'll be worshiping a tree, and in five months she'll have forgotten I ever existed. If I don't make money fast, I can't make her stay.

Dave Mia isn't going to not go to university because you've sold enough Fanta to buy a Vauxhall Corsa.

Aidan But a Lotus Elise, maybe. It's the only hope I've got.

Dave Can't you just, talk to her, isn't that what women like? Talking to them. Can't you just tell her how you feel?

Aidan No, I ent gay. And besides, it's make cash, smash gash, in that order.

We are back online. A muscle gym bro comes on stage.

Muscle Man Yo my guys, welcome to Henchton on the Water, in the county of Swolsbury. Today we are doing dead lifts, let's gooooooo!

Two female police officers struggle to arrest a man, with the man eventually assaulting the woman, while a man films on his phone.

Phone Man This is feminism, this is feminism, this is feminism, this is feminism.

Skip.

A nerdy man enters.

Nerdy Man Look, I know you've heard about drop shipping a million times, and we all know that it is not the best way to make money on Amazon in 2026. But have you heard of release delivery?

Skip.

Someone does a TikTok dance for four seconds – skip.

Skip.

A yoga business muscle man enters.

Yoga Business Muscle Man I was thinking about slavery today, and when you're a slave, you wake up, work all day to make money for your boss, and you do it all day every day. And I thought, if slaves can do it, why can't I?

Skip.

A games reviewer enter the stage.

Games Reviewer Mario Tennis Fever is out now on the Switch 2 and /

Hugo Bang *enters.*

Hugo Bang / Shut up, you fat neek.

Hugo Bang *pushes* **Games Reviewer** *to the floor.* **Games Reviewer** *exits while clutching their arm.*

Games Reviewer Owww, my arm.

Hugo Bang (*speaking directly to* **Aidan**) It's a man's world, it's man v man, men's worlds fight men's worlds, while the little women march to them, outwardly saying no don't fight, but despite everything they say and do, I can tell they actually like it. I know women because I've had sex with twelve of them.

All men come out of the womb like Stone Cold Steve Austin. Breaking through the glass of the vagina. Smashing two beer cans near their face. 'Thank you, mother, now where's my steak?' But the modern world, with the laws and the lesbians and the health and safety. It wants to turn you into someone who politely holds cartons of soy milk near your face, opens glass doors instead of smashing through them like cavemen did, stop stunning mankind to be the best in the world and spend your time playing the Legend of Gay Boy while trying to do silly little scooter tricks.

Vince McMahon and the rest of the billionaires, they already have the money. They've got the houses, and the cars, and the clothes, and the women, sometimes even as many as twelve.

And then there's you who has nothing, literally nothing, less than nothing, no one would care if you died. They want you to be their ass-licking lapdog while they're the cats licky licking up their cream. Dogs should never lick a cat's arse. Not in my world.

Why follow their rules if they don't work for you? That's why they try to make you gay, so you don't stunner their rules. But the rules make you invisible, to employers, to women, to everyone.

No one cares about you, you see that in your life every day, no one gives a damn about you. So why should you give a damn about anyone else? Empathy keeps you invisible. You can care about other people when people start caring about you, and no one will care about you until you've got money.

But I have money, so I'm going to go find lucky number thirteen.

Hugo Bang *exits, as he does, he ruffles* **Aidan***'s hair.*

Scene Three

Aidan *is sat on his phone.* **Mia** *and* **Charlie** *enter.* **Charlie** *is considerably larger than* **Aidan**, *he has a middle parting of freshly washed hair, a slightly unironed blue shirt, chino trousers and Nike trainers. He drapes his arm around* **Mia**.

Mia Hiya.

Aidan Jesus Christ, kill me now.

Charlie Here he is!

Charlie *hugs* **Aidan**.

Charlie So good to finally meet you!

Aidan Yea, so good.

Aidan *starts scooting about, he tries the trick, fails.*

Charlie Mia never shuts up about you!

Aidan She never shuts up in general, women!

Charlie Ironic sexism, very good and funny.

Mia I mentioned you maybe twice.

Charlie Thought you might be her imaginary friend!

Mia Aidan has an imaginary friend, is Ruth here now?

Aidan Charlie doesn't want to hear about Ruth.

Charlie Yes I do. Imagination is a really good skill, corporations are looking for creative minds right now. That's very impressive.

Aidan Buzzing. So, did you bring a scooter or?

Charlie No, I could never do that, I'm just so big and clumsy, you're really lucky being so slight, you can do these fun little games without having all this mass that I have getting in the way. Grrrrr, my excessive bulk.

Aidan *stops scooting.*

Aidan What we doing then?

Mia Chatting.

Aidan Ah right.

Pause as they stand in silence. **Aidan** *does a bunny hop.*

Charlie Whoa, did you see that, Mia, he went up and down.

Mia Yea, mind blown.

Charlie I'll say.

Pause again.

So, you watch much footy, do you?

Aidan Nah.

Charlie Ruggers?

Aidan Nah.

Charlie Cricket?

Aidan Yea mate, big test match fan, me. Me, Tarquin and Horatio are down there every match eating crumpets and shouting six.

Charlie I've never seen you down the county ground.

Mia He's doing one of his jokes, aren't you?

Aidan *smiles.*

Charlie Ha! You are funny. Banter! Mia was saying how funny you are.

Aidan Were you?

Mia Was I?

Charlie You're all she ever talks about, I probably know more about your mum than I do my own.

Aidan Why you talking 'bout my mum?

Mia No I wasn't.

Aidan He wouldn't have said that if you weren't, would he?

Charlie She was only /

Aidan / what you say about my mum?

Mia That she was a nurse.

Charlie It's very complimentary, she wants to take photos of your mum for her portfolio.

Mia Charlie!

Aidan You what?

Mia Do you just say everything you're thinking?

Aidan Why are you taking photos of my mum, what?

Charlie I don't think she meant racy ones.

Mia I was only thinking, I might ask if it's okay, to finish my project, for my course.

Aidan You haven't even gone yet, you might not get in.

Mia I only need three Bs. It's prep work before we start.

Aidan Gagging to leave, ent ya?

Charlie Mia's doing a photography degree, my family are very proud.

Aidan I know that, I bought her her first camera.

Mia Did you?

Aidan Yea I, well, I stole it, the, I got in loads of trouble for that, you don't remember?

Mia When?

Aidan You honestly don't remember?

Mia My dad bought me one when I was eleven.

Aidan No, we were in Year 5, on the school trip to Isle of Wight, in that dinosaur gift shop by the beach, I kegged Harry, to cause a distraction, and he couldn't get his trackies up because that was when he had a broken collarbone from when he got trampled playing bulldog, so the shop lady had to try and help and I stole a disposable camera with a T-rex on it and gave it to you as a present.

Mia Yes! Oh my god! And then Mrs Dennison found out and made you pay for it, but you'd already spent all your money at the service station on the fruit machine, so I had to pay. Good times.

Charlie So Mia bought it really.

Mia No well, technically, but.

Beat.

Aidan Yea, I guess you bought it then.

Charlie You'll love this then, buddy. Show Aidan what I got you for your birthday this year.

Mia Oh don't.

Charlie Get it out.

Aidan What did he get you?

Mia A Canon camera.

Charlie And the lenses. The man on YouTube recommended the lenses. That's what she's going to take photos of your mum with, the camera I bought her, before she goes to university.

Aidan Is she?

Mia Just an idea.

Charlie And what's good is that, when I'm playing in the rugby team she can come and take photos of me. Power couple don't you think, Aidan?

Aidan Where'd you play rugby?

Charlie Old Northamptonians, but I'm going to Bristol too. So I'll be playing for their rugby team hopefully.

Aidan So you're going to Bristol together?

Mia Not going together, but, yea.

Charlie (*to* **Mia**) Oh, I forgot to mention, we can give you a lift down, Rupert's taking the landy.

Mia (*to* **Charlie**) Ah, that's amazing. Oh my god, could we go to Gloucester Services on the way?

Charlie (*to* **Mia**) Rupert's no longer my father if he doesn't go to Gloucester Services.

Aidan Oh right, Mia didn't mention you were going to Bristol too.

Charlie She's too busy talking about you, hey Aidan, celebrity.

Aidan Talks more about me than to me, apparently.

Mia So do you think you'd be okay with that, if I asked your mum?

Aidan She can't do them.

Mia I can do it around her schedule.

Aidan She don't have a schedule, Mia, she's not well.

Mia I know but.

Aidan This ent about you.

Mia I didn't say it was.

Charlie Do it as a going away present.

Aidan I ent going nowhere, she should give me a present, she's the one leaving. Why do you even want to? Take photos of your own mum.

Mia No, that would be boring.

Aidan So would mine.

Mia No it wouldn't, your mum's /

Aidan / What is she?

Mia She's amazing, but in like a, something way, I can't think of the right word.

Charlie Gritty.

Mia That's not /

Aidan / She's not gritty, she likes Snow Patrol. You're not taking photos of my mum.

Mia Well, I have to take photos that represent the reality of where I'm from.

Aidan Why, you just did everything you could to leave.

Mia Aidan, don't start this, Charlie's here.

Aidan So what? No offence, Charlie, but your opinion means nothing to me.

Charlie Your self-confidence is admirable.

Mia People leave and go to university, that's what lots of people do.

Aidan There's a uni here.

Mia But I want to go and experience things, you understand that, right? I'm not leaving you, I'm just going somewhere else.

Aidan Nah, I get it, Northampton ent good enough for Mia cus she's going places but knob head Aidan and his depressed mum can stay and rot, yea that's fine.

Mia I need to take photos of something interesting, something that the lecturers will think captures something important. Your mum's not gritty, she's . . . Do you remember when I used to go to your house and you'd get in a strop and go play in your room by yourself, your mum would always do these funny catwalk shows for me to take photos of. So I wanted to tell that story. Of her, and me. Make it a series of how we both grew as people. I know she's your mum but, she means a lot to me too.

Aidan She's changed.

Mia I know, but I'm not trying to take advantage of her, she's just the most interesting person I know. I get that I haven't seen her in a while, and I'm sorry that she's struggling, but I think she'd enjoy it, Aunty Jones is a diva that needs to have her story told.

Please Aidan, you bought me my first camera, so it's your fault really.

Beat.

Aidan I wanna help, just, I can't like, she's really not, I'm not joking when I say she's not well. You used to take photos of me. So, like, the idea would still work, of us growing as people or whatever, if you took my photo.

Mia Yea?

Charlie You are gritty.

Aidan No I'm not. Yea, just like, me doing scooter tricks and stuff, be great. Look.

Aidan *tries the trick, but fails.*

But you could edit the photo so I land it.

Mia No. Scooting photos aren't going to impress my lecturers. I need to take photos of the real Northampton. Maybe photos of you living your life.

Aidan And what, you just want me to stand there, and what?

Mia Just be.

Beat.

Aidan Be what?

Charlie Be /

Aidan / Don't you say gritty.

Beat.

Charlie Poor?

Mia No, sorry, he, didn't mean that.

Beat.

Aidan You know Mia, she might pretend to be all posh now, but her mum goes to Farmfoods. So don't you start thinking she's like you cus she ent.

Charlie You don't need to feel ashamed, Aidan, my family have struggled too, my little sister started boarding school last summer and we haven't been skiing since.

Mia Stop talking about skiing, please.

Aidan I ain't ashamed, I'm not poor anymore because while you two have been hanging around in reggae bars talking about hummus with idiots, I've been starting a business, I have. And it's going, it's only a week in and we've had some teething problems, but it'll be alright. So you can't take your photos of me, because they wouldn't be photos of your poor old best friend who you pity. They'd be photos of a rich and successful CEO. That's who I am. Screw you and your shiny camera and your massive shoulders and your fluffy hair, I've got work to do.

We go online.

An angry woman enters with a shop assistant.

Angry Woman How dare you! How dare you treat us like this? I have three children and they want ice cream. I have rights! They are in the constitution.

Shop Assistant Miss, we are in Swansea.

An American woman enters.

American Woman Explain this to me. How do you expect me to have a job, when my dog literally has separation anxiety?

Skip.

Donald Trump and Benjamin Netanyahu skip hand-in-hand, feed each other chocolates and kiss, then a baby falls from the sky and a woman screams.

Hugo Bang *enters.*

Hugo Bang So I was with this female who wouldn't shut up, typical. And she mentioned her boyfriend, I left. Why would I waste my time on a female that isn't going to sleep with me? But then I shagged her sister, and the original female, she came back, because that's what they're like. Females need to know you can get other females. They can't think for themselves. They follow the herd. Why do you think you don't get male sheep? Because all females are sheep. Darwin. It's wolves who shag the sheep all night long. That's why top Gs like me get all of them. You gotta shag the females to shag more females. It's a females and egg situation.

Skip.

Games Reviewer *walks on in a cast.*

Games Reviewer Let's look at what April's going to look like for gaming fans /

Hugo Bang *does some sort of wrestling move on* **Games Reviewer**.

Hugo Bang / See this unconscious pile of beta is the problem. This disgusting little cretin thinks he can impress people by following all the rules, he tried hard for his grades, he pays his taxes, he's nice to people. He followed the path he was told to.

And now he's begging me not to hurt him. People like me, people like you, Aidan. Our parents failed us. School failed us. The state failed us. So why would we play their rigged game now? You do whatever you need to make sure this simp beta lies snivelling on the floor and your foot is on his throat. You break their rules, they've never helped you. Because when your heel is crushing their trachea, it's you who gets to make the rules.

Aidan *puts his foot on the throat of the* **Games Reviewer**, *as many women begin to dance around him.*

Scene Four

Aidan *is standing up after giving a presentation to* **Grace**. **Dave** *is standing with a clipboard.* **Grace** *is sat on a skateboard, she's wearing brand new Vans, a Thrasher t-shirt and Dickies chinos.*

Aidan In conclusion, let's grab that bag, any questions?

Grace You're moving mad, you ate with that one, I'm Grace, B.T.W.

Aidan You want a job then?

Grace Not being salty but, is it low key legal?

Aidan My mentor, he says, get rich before you get legal. So let's go in the right order, yea?

Grace Is he your mentor?

Aidan El Davo? Nah, he's my right-hand man.

Grace El Davo? Are you Español?

Dave I'm afraid not señorita, I just happen to be a connoisseur of the lager beer San Miguel and, as the comprehensive education system has failed the youth of this town, they believe putting an el and an o on something makes it seem as if it's coming from the southern peninsula, ergo the children have christened me El Davo. Chin Chin.

Dave *cracks open a can of San Miguel.*

Aidan Yea but, he's got that dog in him so, he's good at business.

Grace Sigma male grindset, that's lit, on god on god no cap.

Beat.

Aidan Yea exactly, anything else?

Grace Yea, mad thankful that you gave me a hella long business presentation, but I just came to the skatepark to lock in and skate.

Aidan Yea, I used to be like you, lost, alone, wasting my time on pointless tasks, invisible to the world, skating away my days.

Aidan *tries the trick, fails.*

But it ends in failure every time. See, I remember this time, back before I became the alpha I am today, before I started Northampton's hottest new delivery service, Alpha Mail, but spelt like Royal Mail, and I was stacking shelves in Mortimer's till my fingers bled, my knees weak, arms bent.

Grace Mum's spaghetti.

Aidan No, it was baba ganoush. And during yet another one of the worst days of my life, this female she comes up to me, and I'll always remember what she said, it was, what was it, Davorroney?

Dave (*as if rehearsed*) I don't know, Aidan. Tell us.

Aidan She said. (**Aidan** *takes a moment as if he is holding back his emotions.*) She looked deep into my eyes, into my soul and said, 'Do you know where the Old El Paso fajita kits are?' Because they don't care about us. We are nothing to them, we are the bringers of salsa and tortillas in a cardboard box and nothing more. We need to put our skateboards down and become the alphas that they don't want us to be.

Beat.

Grace No doubt, but, if we are trying to be business-coded, why are we in a skatepark? I get aesthetic but, aren't businesses that make hella skrilla usually giving office?

Aidan Yea, they are, normally, giving office, but, it's about, being adaptable and in the moment you know what I mean. And er, offices cost loads of money, skrilla, and you have to buy stuff to go into coffee shops. And the library is full of people shouting about their benefits being cancelled. So this is the only free place to go.

Grace Radlands is pretty Gucci.

Dave No, I think it's council.

Grace Council, ain't it, chief.

Aidan Yea, that's what I'm always saying. El Davo, your shift is starting, so you better head off, yea, and don't just try and sell Bovril this time, get things people actually want.

Dave Absolutely boss, I'll give Turkish delight a go. Nice to meet you, Grace.

Grace Bet.

Dave No darling, I don't need another addiction.

Dave *leaves.*

Beat.

Grace I'm glad I came. Cus low key not sipping hot tea but, because this place is in Northampton, I assumed it would be cheugy as. Not to drag, but, it's actual bougie.

Aidan Good?

Grace Stan the based non flexing zady.

Beat.

Aidan No offence, but I have no idea what you're on about like ninety per cent of the time. Can't you just speak well normal, en it.

Grace No cap, that's high key cringe, was I, ah no I'm giving highlighter kid, you got my ass, I'm dead, you've killed me, you're giving Dahmer. Sorry.

Aidan Am I?

Grace What, ew oh god I'm so cringe, I can't look. I thought everyone spoke like this who doesn't go to my school. I'm crashing out, sorry. I'll talk normally and stop yap trapping. Sorry, I'm just a girl. Fuck!

Aidan Are you okay?

Grace Big yikes, (*Really trying to speak normally.*) Yes, I, am, having, a, splendid, day, how, is, your, day, friend?

Aidan What school do you go to?

Grace I'm not really from here, well I kind of am, not really, I, I go to boarding school.

Aidan Buy us a Monster then.

Grace I'm low key not actually that bougie though, my family actually have no skrilla left after paying my guap school fees. (*Realising she's gone back into her previous vernacular.*) I'm a walking ick, I hate myself.

Aidan Nah, I ent having a go, I like rich people.

Grace No, I'm a hella Marx stan, big Marx fan, sorry.

Aidan That's how you can tell if someone's got proper money, if they got a trolley out at Marks and Spencer.

Grace Karl Marx, I simp for socialism. (**Grace** *decides that phrase is okay.*)

Aidan I prefer Percy Pigs. I'm going to send my kids to private school.

Grace They wouldn't even learn anything though, the vibes are so off, it has no aura. It's bad. You constantly have to be locked in.

Aidan They lock you in? Oh sorry, that's just like concentrating, right?

Grace No, like, lock us in, behind a big gate.

Aidan Why?

Grace Otherwise we escape, and then we are late for lessons and get put in the tardy book.

Aidan Your school has a retard book? That's a bit harsh.

Grace No, it's a list for people who are late. That's not TikTok, that's just posh.

Aidan At college my teacher thought I was called Arthur. Reckon you could start this week?

Grace Oh okay, bet, I didn't realise I got the job, thanks. I'll probably have to borrow my brother's phone, I got a brick. I am going away in like a month and a half though.

Aidan Ah what, you're going to Bristol with a rugby player un all?

Grace No, Cheltenham. I was kind of hoping to wildflower, sorry. Have a hot girl summer, sorry I can't really translate that one. Thing is I don't really know anyone from the town.

Aidan You can focus on your work then, make some money.

Grace I was hoping someone might show me around.

Aidan Ah yea, well delivering will help you get to know everything. They should do like, a tour, maybe Google it?

Grace But one giving a personal touch.

Aidan Ah well, hope you find someone.

Beat.

Grace Big yikes.

Beat.

Aidan Ah, you meant me. Sorry, I've got erm, slow processing apparently. But yea erm, right, okay. Here is the 'Aidan tour of Northampton'. Down there you can get the X6 to Milton Keynes.

Grace Great tour, bud.

Aidan (*to self*) Sheep.

Grace What?

Beat.

Aidan You want a Yum Yum Peanut Butter Jam Jam Glory Deluxe?

Grace Cheffin, sorry, where do you get them from?

Aidan I get the ingredients from Mortimer's, I buy them in bulk and then I make them here.

Grace Much love, to you for giving me this.

She bites one.

Oh these are bussin', lovely.

Aidan That's £7.99.

Grace Oh, bet, yea that's deluxe.

Aidan Yea.

Grace Do you work at Mortimer's?

Aidan (*sarcastically*) Well done, Darwin, no I just wear the staff uniform to look cool.

Grace No cap, I mean, cool dude, sorry.

Aidan No of course I work there, you numpty.

Grace I oop. No need to drag me so hard, Jesus Christ, Grace, I know some boys that wear like, McDonald's hats or like, Greggs' track suits when they don't work there, kinda anti bougie slay but in a not me sounding cringe way.

Aidan That's dumb.

Grace Yea well, I really like Mortimer's.

Aidan Give over, Waitrose.

Grace I like the pizzas, they're buss, (*She stops herself midway.*) fantastic.

Aidan Want to know something about Mortimer's massive pizzas?

Grace Yea.

Aidan You're sworn to secrecy though. If anyone finds out the Mortimer's elite squad team will take you out.

Grace On god.

Aidan No one buys them.

Grace Okay.

Aidan No but I mean like, no one buys them. We've sold one in the last three years, and that one was bought as a joke, they found it in the Nene.

Grace So why do you sell them?

Aidan Wrong question, we aren't trying to sell them. They're subliminal advertising. No one buys Mortimer's massive pizzas but they know about them, they've heard about 'em, they think about them.

Grace I think about them all the time.

Aidan Why are they so big? Why are there so many? People do get obsessed by Mortimer's massive pizzas. They stick around in their head for days, weeks, months, years, lifetimes. People can't sleep, can't concentrate at work, can't get erections, forget to eat all because they are obsessed with Mortimer's massive pizzas.

Grace You're taking the mick, sorry, I didn't get that you /

Aidan / There have been like four divorces where the reason has been 'can't stop talking about Mortimer's massive pizzas'.

Grace Honestly?

Beat.

Aidan No, you div. They're just quite big pizzas.

Grace I'm dead, you are so funny.

Aidan They are big though.

Grace You should do TikToks, you'd be so good.

Aidan Nah, I don't follow the path of sheep. I'm making my business because it'll be my passive income.

Grace Passive incomes are great because I hate doing things.

Aidan Exactly, the only things I like doing are, like, business, but passively.

Grace Yea, business is fun, work hard play hard.

Aidan Yea, mostly working hard right now.

Grace We could play hard.

Beat.

Aidan . . .

Pause.

Aidan Ah yea?

Grace I've got a free house, so, we can play hard there.

Beat.

Aidan Oh erm, right okay, I, er, I've got my Switch in my bag, and a few games downloaded, so like Mario Kart? Mario Party? I've got Smash Bros.

Grace Or we could smash, bro.

Beat.

Aidan Does that mean?

Grace Have sex.

Aidan Oh right yea, cool, cool cool cool, that is what I thought it meant but it's best to like confirm these things you know. Consent. Yea, we could have sex. Or like one life each on Tears of the Kingdom, I've got loads of elixirs, either or really, up to you. I'll bring the Switch anyway, just in case, for after, or, before, not during, probably, well it's already in my bag, so I have to bring it, I could leave it here but don't want to just leave it under a bush. Might rain, doesn't look like rain but you never know, not a farmer. Am I alright to bring my bag? I'll take my shoes off when I come inside.

Carpets. You probably got wooden floor, ent ya.

Back into the internet **Hugo Bang** *enters.*

Hugo Bang Screw you, gobble my knob, I was right.

Aidan Mate.

Hugo Bang Gobble my knob!

Aidan Mate.

Hugo Bang Knob.

Aidan Yea, but no but mate.

Hugo Bang Gobble my /

Aidan / Mate.

Hugo Bang This is it, you see, you listen to them your whole life and where does it get you?

Aidan Nothing.

Hugo Bang Nothing, dead, nothing, dumb, virgin, dumb little dead nothing virgin Aidan. That's what they all called you.

Aidan Er.

Hugo Bang And then you listen to me /

Aidan / Yea but who was calling me that though?

Hugo Bang Listen to me and what happens.

Aidan Not dumb little dead nothing virgin Aidan.

Hugo Bang No longer.

Aidan I'm not sure anyone was actually calling me that though, were they?

Hugo Bang Gobble my knobble.

Aidan Do you actually want me to give you head though? Because I don't really want to and I've got a girlfriend I'm sorry.

Hugo Bang No, my young prince, my prodigy, my child of tomorrow. You don't have a girlfriend. You can't be friends with a girl. A lion isn't friends with a gazelle. A bear isn't friends with a salmon. So how can a man be friends with a female? All you have is one female who is giving all of herself to you, but you know what happens now?

Aidan Is this when Mia wants to go out with me? Because before you were saying if I have sex with someone else, then Mia would want to be my girlfriend.

Hugo Bang You get females because you have money, which gets you more females, the females see you are a male who gets females and they come around, the Pied Piper of pussy, more females, more money and females and female money and monied females you understand? That's power.

And now you claim that power for yourself. And build more of it, so you are 'them'. No more relying on bosses, or government or charities or being part of the community. You are the community, a community of money and females.

Make cash, smash gash.

Hugo Bang *hands over a tin of chewing tobacco.*

Aidan, it's time, join me.

Aidan *takes a bite of chewing tobacco.*

The full ensemble of actors including **Aidan** *perform the dance routine of 'Money' by Lisa. The song continues through the montage with multiple members of the ensemble continuing to dance to it.*

Mia *phones* **Aidan** *from across the stage.*

Mia I'll go with you.

Aidan I don't need to pick my results up, my business is smashing it, money doesn't check qualifications. There is one thing you can do for me. Take some promo shots.

Mia Why would I? I asked you to take photos and you wouldn't do that.

Aidan Well now I'm asking you to take photos, but now, of me, as the CEO of Alpha Mail Incorporated. But not for your stupid portfolio of art, for my LinkedIn. LinkedIn is a . . .

Mia I know what LinkedIn is, so I don't get anything for my project?

Aidan Unless you're doing National Geographic, because you'd just be taking photos of a lion.

Charlie Put Aidan on speaker, you alright geezer, it's your boy Charlie.

Aidan Why are you there?

Charlie We are packing to go on a mini break to Venice. Have you been? Where could we get the best gnocchi?

Mia I can do the photos next Saturday.

Aidan I heard Venice is shit, bye.

Spicy Swine *walks on stage.*

Spicy Swine I'm Spicy Swine and I love meth and hitting the griddy.

Spicy Swine *leaves the stage.*

Hugo Bang *puts* **Spicy Swine** *in a headlock.*

Hugo Bang See Krav Maga, that's what really makes a man, you can have all the money in the world, but what's going to change your mindset, into a wisdom set, is knowing that you are able to choke someone out at a moment's notice.

Aidan*'s on the phone.*

Aidan Mum, I got a lot on, yea I'll do it later. Can't you just grow up and do something for yourself for once? Jesus fucking Christ, do you know who I am?

Two people with substance abuse issues fight each other while someone eats a Cornetto. The Jet2holiday slogan plays.

Hugo Bang *is playing dominoes.*

Hugo Bang All the greats played dominoes, because dominoes is like life, everyone can pick up a piece of plastic with some dots on, but not everyone knows the rules of dominoes. Think about it.

More dancing.

Grace *is on a scooter,* **Aidan** *approaches her.*

Aidan What do you think you're doing?

Grace Caught in 4k literally being a crackhead whore pick-me simp learning a trick to gas my snack.

Grace *does the scooter trick.*

I learnt that trick you've been trying to /

Aidan / Why do you think I'd care, you're meant to be working.

Grace I just thought.

Aidan Don't.

Grace Yikes.

Grace *leaves.*

Hugo Bang You see that? That is what power brings you. That woman is so obsessed with you, she's on that scooter all night doing what Daddy tells her to. Treat them mean to keep them keen. There's two types of men in this world, men that neg and men who get pegged. And there ain't nothing going in our arses.

A man in one of those horrible American suits enters the stage.

Man in One of Those Horrible American Suits But, but, but, can you riddle me this, what is a woman? No, exactly! Libtard owned. (*The man barks three times.*)

Hugo Bang *and* **Aidan** *are making a campfire.*

Hugo Bang It's important to get out into nature to really connect to what matters, even when I'm working on my grindminister lifestyle, I like to get out into the elements. That's why we came out to the racecourse, and really take in what God has given us.

A gross man enters the stage.

Theo Grossman The homeless problem here is sickening. There are children here, disgusting. Oi. Oi, excuse me, excuse me! Why are you homeless? Oi, answer me, why are you homeless? The country's gone. I'm moving to Dubai where there is no poverty at all, apart from the slaves but that's fine.

Dave *and* **Aidan** *speak.*

Aidan I've had it up to here with you, Dave, see I thought that you had that dog in you, but the dog in you is just some miniature poodle, or like, some dopey fat greyhound, I need a terrier, eating rats and chasing cats.

Dave I'm truly trying, Aidan, but I don't have the joie de vivre for a sales based /

Aidan / Excuses are for the weak. And if someone wants to be a part of Aidan's army, they can't be weak. An army marches as fast as their slowest soldier, so if someone is limping, you shoot them in the head. I'm not going to let you drag me down to your level. Improve your numbers or you'll be a dumb nothing dead virgin all your life.

Dave *exits.*

The entire chorus hit the griddy.

Hugo I have never been prouder in my life.

Aidan I'm just trying to be like you, fam.

Hugo Some are born great, some achieve greatness, and some fucking buy it. You take those feelings, you spit them out, and you be everything you have ever dreamed of. The world is ours, you are they. You make the rules that the others follow. The betas look to you for guidance. You are the alpha. You are a top G like me.

Aidan *addresses the audience.*

Aidan You're sat there staring at your misery screens
Hoping it feeds you a morsel of joy.
So you won't ever have to turn them off
And think how bad that your life really is.

You're depressed, you're ugly, you're unhealthy
You're gay, you're poor, you're a fucking virgin
But me I don't see what the world's made you
I envision the you that you'll become.

You're brave, you're strong, you're valiant young men
Who won't lie down when the world tells you to
We can't open doors, when we've bent the knee
Today we stand, we show them who we are
We're no longer trapped in their web of help
Making us need them, so they control us.

Let's break the shackles and claim what is ours
Now we make the cash, and we smash the gash
Now we grab the bag and we shag the slag.
Now we create our own economy.
And we bend over that yummy mummy
We won't be lamenting for yesterday.
No hoping for a better tomorrow
Today is now here, it is our day.
Today is the day they acknowledge me.

Scene Six

Aidan *is now wearing an ill-fitting suit, an undone tie and the bottom button of the suit done up.* **Hugo Bang** *lingers.*

Mia *and* **Charlie** *enter,* **Mia** *is carrying camera equipment and* **Charlie** *is wearing a Venice tourist t-shirt.*

Mia When did you start rehearsals for Bugsy Malone?

Aidan What?

Charlie *sings the first line to 'Bad Guys' from Bugsy Malone.*

Hugo Bang He's trying to usurp you by singing musical numbers, show your dominance.

Mia Your suit is /

Aidan / designer.

Mia T K Maxx?

Aidan I have an eye for a bargain, that's how you can tell I'm genuinely wealthy, because I don't splash the money around, you know. It's classy.

Charlie Absolutely, you look fantastic, do you want some help with the . . .

Aidan Nah I, I can do it, I watched a tutorial, I /

Mia / Just let him, Aidan, not your fault our school used clip-ons.

Charlie It is tricky, Rupert spent forever teaching me.

Charlie *goes over to* **Aidan**, *and like a father helping a son teaches him how to do the tie.*

Charlie (*while doing* **Aidan**'*s tie*) In my house there's a cat and a mouse, as the cat naps, the mouse scurries past, the cat awakes and a chase takes place, the cat jumps up with dinner in sight, and around the chair as the mouse hides, the cat crawls up then peeks inside, wiggle as it might the poor cat is stuck tight. There we go my handsome boy.

Aidan Thanks.

Mia Very demure, very mindful, (*Getting her camera ready.*) would you mind if I used these for my portfolio?

Aidan But how would that work? I look great now?

Charlie Go from a lower angle so he looks taller.

Mia All right, Charlie, I've got the photos bit.

Charlie Okay okay, don't get in the way of an artist and their work, sorry famous feminist photographer Constance Fox Talbot. (*To* **Aidan**.) I read a book. Oh buddy, your bottom button's done up.

Aidan What?

Charlie On your jacket, the bottom button.

Aidan What about it.

Charlie It's done up.

Aidan Yea.

Charlie Yea.

Beat.

Aidan So.

Charlie Sorry it's, it's not meant to be.

Aidan What?

Charlie You don't do the bottom button of a suit jacket up.

Aidan What?

Hugo Bang Really?

Charlie Three button blazer, top to bottom, sometimes, always, never.

Mia He's right.

Aidan Why?

Charlie The king was fat.

Aidan Oh right, fat king was he? So I just leave it undone yea?

Aidan *undoes his button.*

Charlie No, just undo the bottom one, leave the middle one done up, and the top one that's up to you. Individualism. Although obviously when you sit down you undo all of them. Unless you're sat on a horse, when you're sat on a horse standing rules apply.

Aidan *undoes his bottom button.*

Hugo Bang He's them, he is definitely them, you're meant to be them now, Aidan. You be them.

Charlie And next time don't wear white socks with a suit.

Aidan Right.

Charlie Your lapels are a little twisted.

Aidan Just take the picture.

Charlie It needs to be right.

Hugo Bang He's trying to usurp you, you need to prove your dominance, get your penis out.

Aidan Just take the picture, yea?

Mia Charlie is being really helpful.

Aidan Move your finger up and down, that's all you have to do, clicky clicky, do your job, I've got to do mine.

Mia Well unless you want some like 'Aidan's day at the magistrates' office', you should let him sort you out.

Aidan I don't look like I'm in court.

Mia You look like a pimp's assistant who is about to be sentenced to eighty hours' community service. My lecturers will love it.

Charlie You can take the boy out of the estate, but you can't take the estate out of the boy.

Grace *enters,* **Aidan** *rushes over to* **Grace**.

Grace Yo.

Aidan Sup bitch! Yo Mia meet /

Charlie My sister!

Aidan *stops in his tracks.*

Mia Oh my god, you're the amazing Grace!

Grace Most people just call me the average Grace, so you're Mia then. Charlie, you should have mentioned how pretty she is.

Mia No shut up, you're really pretty.

Hugo Bang Pathetic females.

Grace Sorry we haven't met.

Mia No, you've been at school, and then you seem to have been out the whole summer?

Charlie Ha, how lucky am I, Aidan? A beautiful girlfriend and a wonderful sister. Life is great.

Mia Aidan, do you know Grace?

Aidan . . . Nah.

Mia Because you said, 'Sup bitch' to her.

Aidan Yea, that's just how I talk to females . . . bitch.

Hugo Bang That's my boy.

Mia No it's not.

Charlie Well, I'd appreciate it if you don't call my sister and girlfriend bitches, but Grace, meet my good friend and ally Aidan.

Aidan Nice to meet you, Amy was it?

Grace What are you doing?

Aidan What do you mean?

Grace Why are you pretending you don't know me? My brother won't mind.

Charlie Mind what?

Grace Me and Aidan are /

Aidan / She works for me.

Hugo Bang Tell the truth, you coward! A gentleman always shags and brags.

Charlie How fantastic. It's like you have a paper round, very retro!

Aidan It's not a paper round, it's a legitimate business.

Mia Well, it can't be that legitimate if you're employing fourteen-year-olds.

Beat.

Aidan You what?

Grace Yea but, I'm a mature fourteen-year-old.

Charlie She really is, my parents have been letting her stay at home alone without a nanny this summer. So tell me, Grace, what is it like working for the CEO of looking-cooler-than-a-cucumber-in-his-new-suit Aidan.

Grace Well, we aren't just co-workers.

Mia Really?

Aidan Well, I want my employees to see Alpha Mail Incorporated like a family, but one with an alpha male.

Hugo Bang Why are you denying yourself the honour of being a top G, be proud of your conquests.

Grace Aidan, why are you being weird?

Aidan I'm not being weird, you're being weird.

Mia You are being weird.

Charlie A little unusual.

Aidan What am I doing that's weird?

Grace Well, you're pretending that you aren't my boyfriend.

Aidan Your what! Grace, you . . . you . . . funny girl . . . You're being stupid. It's one of her jokes.

Hugo Bang Be proud, fucking someone's sister is a perfect way to assert your authority.

Charlie I don't understand.

Aidan I . . . I . . . I have no idea what you are on about.

Grace I can't believe you would act like this after you took my virginity.

Beat.

Charlie No.

Mia You had sex with her?

Aidan I don't know . . .

Hugo Bang She was gagging for it.

Aidan She basically begged me for it.

Mia She's a child, Aidan.

Grace No I'm not.

Mia Legally you are, you can't consent.

Grace Don't patronise me, I wanted to.

Mia That's statutory rape.

Aidan Nah nah nah.

Hugo Bang Typical liberal wokerati drumming up fake news to take down successful men.

Charlie You raped my sister.

Mia After everything I went through and now you do this, honestly Aidan.

Aidan No, I ain't like that guy.

Mia You are.

Charlie I'm calling the police.

Grace No don't.

Charlie You might not understand this now, but what he has done to you is very wrong.

Aidan Charlie, please don't call them, please.

Grace No we, we love each other so, it's fine.

Aidan Please don't call the police, it will ruin me.

Charlie Should I call them Mia?

Mia Why's it my decision?

Aidan I didn't know she was fourteen.

Mia How did you not know?

Aidan I don't check ID.

Charlie I'm going to call the police.

Grace No stop please. I'll say it never happened.

Mia Grace, you, you can't lie about these kinds of things but, Aidan, how can I defend you for this? What am I meant to do now?

Aidan Please don't.

Grace Please.

Mia If Grace is going to lie, there's not much you can do.

Charlie Don't think you've got out of this.

He puts down the phone.

Hugo Bang I'm sick of you acting like you're a dumb nothing virgin bitch again, Aidan.

Grace I'm not a victim, we love each other, don't we, Aidan?

Aidan Well, it's not like, that serious.

Grace Are you joking?

Hugo Bang What did she expect? You can't be tied down to one woman.

Aidan You know, I can't be tied down to one woman, that's what you signed up for, you date an alpha and /

Grace / I can't believe this.

Grace *starts crying.*

Charlie If you loved her then maybe.

Mia No, still no.

Charlie But if you're going to be cruel to her.

Aidan Then what?

Mia Are you okay, Grace?

Grace I just want to go home.

Mia You see what you've done?

Hugo Bang A female crying, big deal.

Aidan It's not like making a girl cry is a big deal, you guys cry over anything.

Charlie You better watch yourself.

Grace I literally worked all summer delivering takeaways on a scooter, why did you think I was doing that?

Hugo Bang You got paid.

Aidan You got paid.

Grace I don't need money, I just wanted someone to be with.

Hugo Bang Well, you should have found a /

Aidan / Well, you should have found a beta male simp. That's not me.

Mia This isn't you.

Aidan *and* **Hugo Bang** You don't know me.

Charlie I do, you are vermin.

Aidan *and* **Hugo Bang** (*a growing chorus of* **Hugo Bang***s say this line*) Yea I am, call the police, that's what you wanted to do the second you saw me anyway. That's all I am to you, I either have to learn how to do my buttons up the right way so I can be exactly like you or I get sent off to prison.

Mia Because you are a rapist.

Aidan *and* **Hugo Bang** (*a growing chorus of* **Hugo Bang***s say this line*) Oh that's convenient for you, the second I start to become successful I'm suddenly a criminal. You can try to exterminate me all you like, but you can't get rid of vermin.

Charlie Apologise to my sister.

Aidan *and* **Hugo Bang** (*a large chorus of* **Hugo Bang***s say this line*) Go fuck yourself.

Hugo Bang *spits on* **Charlie**.

Charlie *pushes* **Aidan** *to the ground,* **Charlie** *climbs on top of* **Aidan**, *raises his fist. A* **Hugo Bang** *appears.*

Mia Just leave him.

And another two **Hugo Bang***s appear.*

Grace Please don't, let's just go.

Charlie You're lucky I'm not scum like you.

Charlie *looks at* **Aidan**, *lets go of him and turns away. One of the* **Hugo Bang***s passes* **Aidan** *the scooter,* **Aidan** *goes to hit* **Charlie** *but he doesn't. A few more* **Hugo Bang***s appear.*

One of the **Hugo Bang***s snatches the scooter from* **Aidan** *and hits* **Charlie** *over the head. Blood splatters over* **Aidan**.

A Chorus de Bang swarm the stage. They attack **Charlie**. **Aidan** *steps back watching the Chorus de Bang batter* **Charlie**. **Aidan** *joins in and starts attacking* **Charlie**.

The Chorus de Bang back away from **Charlie**.

Dave *rushes in and pulls* **Aidan** *off* **Charlie**. **Grace** *and* **Mia** *hold* **Charlie** *and exit.*

Aidan *stands covered in blood.*

Aidan Yea, you better run! Go on, jog on. Come back and see what you get! I'll mash you up! Suck my dick, you bitch!

Dave Are you okay?

Aidan I'm the boss! I'm the fucking big boss man!

Dave Yes but, you're /

Aidan / Look at me. Look at me!

Dave I am.

Aidan What do you see?

Dave A boy covered in blood.

Aidan What? Nah, it ain't my blood. It's that bitch's blood.

Dave Oh, is that better?

Aidan Spoils of war. (*Shouting again to* **Charlie**.) Who's they now! Who's they now! I'll do whatever buttons up I want. I'm the fat king. Fat king, big dick swinging, bitch!

Dave Why were you attacking him?

Aidan It was a fight, I won.

Dave That's not what I saw.

Aidan I don't start fights, I finish them.

Dave You hit him in the back of the head as he was walking away.

Aidan Yea, like a lion. That's how wolves hunt. Fuck off, you gimp. I'm hard as fuck. Suck my dick.

Dave And I suppose you're proud of yourself.

Aidan Lions don't worry about the opinion of sheep.

Dave And you're the lion in this scenario?

Aidan Fucking king of the jungle, hakuna matata.

Dave You're the alpha?

Aidan Comes natural.

Dave So then where is your pride?

Aidan Well, they had to help Charlie because he's a little pussy! Thought he was a big man, but he ent shit when it comes to real world economics /

Dave / I believe an alpha is only an alpha if they have a pack who follow them. If your pack left with Charlie, that would make him the alpha.

Aidan Nah because he lost the fight, I smashed him up /

Dave / The girls don't seem to mind.

Aidan Yea cus, well, I'm sigma then, that's more based anyway, and the girls have that woke mind virus that's going round, and it's probably infected their senses and, microplastics, the vaccine, they have changed them. They can't even tell when a real man is in front of them. That's why they've done it.

Dave You've done your research.

Aidan Yea, like, that's why like, we had shit lives, cus they want to keep us down, and then they can have all the women while we fight each other.

Dave It's a possibility.

Aidan What, you believe what they want you to? Thought you were better than that.

Dave I didn't say that.

Aidan You're going to believe people that think jet fuel melts steel beams?

Dave I might well believe you.

Aidan You better, look around you, like, that's what keeps you down, and me and my mum. It's them.

Dave There are systems which don't work to our advantage.

Aidan Yea, like, we have no choices.

Dave You do have choices.

Aidan Nah, like, I didn't like, choose to do that, like with Grace, and then Charlie. That wasn't me. That was them. They made me with their ways.

Dave No.

Aidan Nah, it can't be me, because if it's me then, your life is your fault as well so, it's them.

Dave I'm an alcoholic.

Aidan Well yea, that's how they control you. Poisoned your mind with alcohol.

Dave I have a criminal record.

Aidan So they track you, keep tabs on you. What don't you get about this? This is how they do it. It's not our fault!

Dave I hit a pedestrian while drink driving, Aidan.

Beat.

Aidan Because they made you drink.

Dave No one can make you do anything. I chose to drink. I then chose to drive, I then killed a little boy, that was me.

Aidan Because.

Dave My life as you see it is the consequence of my actions.

Aidan Well, yea but I only did what I was told, like, I followed advice, like, I was making myself a better man.

Dave You chose to follow advice. You made that choice.

Aidan No because, like, you said there's a system that's designed to keep me being shit.

Dave None of that means you can assault people.

Aidan I'm the victim.

Dave I thought you were a lion. You need to pick one.

Aidan You're being a twat.

Dave I'm treating you like the man you're trying to be.

Aidan I am a man.

Dave You're a coward.

Aidan I'm not a fucking coward. Look at everything I've done.

Dave Then take responsibility for it! We can't go around pretending we have no say in how our lives are lived. Not every criminal is secretly a tortured poet who has been misunderstood and manipulated. People do bad things to people, and they should face the consequences. It must be incredibly comforting for you to believe the world is out to get you. You can blame society for forcing you into nefarious arms, then blame nefarious arms when you commit their nefarious deeds. It was you, nothing more, nothing less.

Aidan You're them.

Dave Everyone's them.

Aidan I didn't mean to.

Dave You didn't do it by accident.

Aidan I didn't want to.

Dave And yet you did it.

Aidan Yea well, at least I didn't kill some kid.

Dave That 'some kid' I killed was my son.

Aidan Oh.

Dave I just, you're the same age he'd of been . . . If he hadn't . . . If I hadn't . . . I thought I might be able to help you. I was mistaken. I didn't know it would end this way. I wanted you to be better than me. I failed. I'm sorry.

Aidan I'm sorry.

Dave No, don't be sorry, be better.

Beat.

Aidan How?

Dave If I had those answers, I wouldn't be drinking lager at the skatepark with a teenager. I've got as far as knowing it's my fault. How to make it better? That's on you.

Aidan Can I have one?

Dave I'm not giving you something else to blame.

Aidan *picks up his phone, he chooses not to look at it. The Chorus de Bang undress* **Aidan** *from his suit, and redress him in his original costume.*

Scene Seven

Aidan *is sat down rocking on his scooter.* **Mia** *walks in.*

Mia You left me on read for like, two weeks.

Aidan Oh, yea, I haven't been using my phone.

Mia Because of . . .?

Aidan 'For you' got a bit . . .

Mia Yea, just a bit.

Aidan How's Charlie doing?

Mia He's fine. You aren't getting caught I'm afraid. I begged Charlie not to call the police. So much that Charlie got kind of jealous, we broke up actually. But it's okay, I'll get over it.

Aidan He was nice, nicer than me.

Mia Yea, he was, but, he always wanted to go on walks, just these really long walks constantly, like not walking to anywhere just walking. Posh people just love walking around for no reason, it's genuinely mental.

Aidan Yea, and he was probably too big. Like, I'm a good size, but he's freakishly tall, it's abnormal.

Mia Yea, he was really handsome.

Aidan In like a, really conventional way.

Mia In a handsome way.

Aidan But like, you're not with him anymore?

Mia Nope.

Aidan Because you fought for me to be okay too much?

Mia I guess.

Aidan So, do you want to go out with me instead?

Pause.

Mia Are you fucking kidding me! You have gone literally mental, I swear.

Aidan Oh this is typical of /

Mia / No! No! Fuck you, Aidan. Are you that deluded that you think I would start falling in love with you because I see you take advantage of some legal child who was obviously in love with you and then you hit my boyfriend round the head with a scooter?

Aidan Oh just get me arrested then.

Mia You have no idea how much I fought for you. I said all of this about how you were manipulated and how you didn't know and how you were a good person. I shouldn't have bothered.

Aidan Then why did you?

Mia Because you're my friend.

Aidan But I don't want to just be friends.

Mia So what? What do you want to do? You want to get your dick wet and then what, be exactly the same? We see each other all the time.

Aidan No we don't.

Mia Not as much as we used to but.

Aidan And you're leaving.

Mia You thought I'd stay to be with you?

Aidan I hoped you would.

Mia Well I'm not, I got in, so I'm going.

Aidan Well done.

Mia Yea.

Aidan I'm happy for you.

Mia Thank you.

Beat.

Aidan You'll have this life and I'll just, stay here.

Mia You've got your business.

Aidan Ha yea, people wrote reviews saying we were selling stuff on the side so DeliverEats fired me. And Mortimer's realised I was reselling using my staff discount, so they fired me unall.

Mia Right.

Aidan So after everything, I'm left with a massive suit that's covered in blood, a fake Rolex with a smashed face, three boxes of Turkish delight and a crate of Vimto. Share?

Mia Yea.

They eat the Turkish delight and drink the Vimto.

Mia Have you spoken to Grace?

Aidan Nah, she'll be better off if she forgets I ever existed.

Mia She won't ever forget you.

Aidan Shame for her.

Mia Did you genuinely not know how old she was?

Aidan Honest like, literally, I know nothing about her.

Mia I'm sorry but, you did know, maybe she never said but, she seemed fourteen. Like, you just didn't want to know in case you didn't like what you found out.

Aidan I wasn't interested in her.

Mia That's kind of worse. Like, the only thing about her you thought was worth learning, was if she'd have sex with you.

Beat

Horrifying.

Aidan I was trying to work on myself.

Mia But Grace is a person, like she's got thoughts and feelings, it's not just about you.

Aidan I just wanted, I thought that this summer would be about me, and it was, and that's why it's gone so badly. I was only going out with her to try and impress you anyway.

Mia How fucking dare you. Don't try to blame this on me. Even if she wasn't a kid. You fucked some random, broke their heart, and I'm going to be like, 'yea that's the man I want to spend my life with'.

Aidan Not like that.

Mia What really gets me is you know what I went through when I was Grace's age.

Aidan No, I'm nothing like him.

Mia Well he was eighteen, so.

Aidan Yea but, I'm not like him.

Mia To Grace you are. And kind of to me, now. She won't be able to forget that. Thing is, you made her a victim. And she'll be great, I'm sure she can overcome what you've done to her. But you'll linger, for her whole life, and when she least expects it, when she's feeling beaten down, or low, or just random times, the memory of you, and what you did will be there. Haunting her.

Aidan I'll leave her alone now.

Mia Doesn't matter, people don't forget that. The first time she ever had sex with someone was rape. She doesn't get some big recovery, no revenge, no vengeance, the police wouldn't do anything even if she wanted them to. Grace is the one who has to deal with everything, while you just get to carry on with your life.

Beat.

Aidan Am I a bad person?

Mia Change. Be better.

Aidan Maybe it's all downhill from here, like I'm one of those people who peaked in school.

Mia You were awful in school.

Aidan Oh mate, even my peak was rubbish. I'm a human mole hill. I'm not trying to, like, make you like me again or anything, I just. You're right. I am sorry. To Grace, and you.

Mia And Charlie.

Aidan Yea, I'm sorry.

Mia I know, I wish you were going somewhere.

Aidan I like Northampton, well, it's alright, it's average you know, it's actually like the most average place that you could make. It suits me.

Mia Are you actually going to be okay? I'm a bit worried about you.

Aidan Don't be, like, it is what it is, you know. I tried to have the money and the women and retire by forty, and I failed.

Mia You're eighteen.

Aidan Yea but like, you can go to uni and try to be a photographer, but if you fail you can just do something else that'll get you a job. And then you can mess up but, you'll just keep getting chances. Chance after chance until you end up succeeding at something. People like you end up alright. But for me, I've just been fired from DeliverEats and a supermarket. There's nowhere else to go.

Mia You thought of an idea, it was illegal, and then you messed it up by being more illegal, but you just have to think of a legal one and you'll be fine.

Aidan So what am I supposed to do?

Mia Literally no one knows, but don't just blame women because they don't like you, we are all just twats trying our best.

Aidan I tried at the business and failed, and then didn't put any effort in on the course and ended up scraping a merit, weird.

Mia Well done.

Aidan Most people get a distinction or whatever, but still, didn't fail.

Mia So you could go to uni?

Aidan No.

Mia I mean not like, a good uni obviously, or even an average one, but, you could go to a uni that let in pretty much everyone. Northampton!

Aidan I'm pretty much everyone.

Mia I can't tell if you're joking.

Aidan No, right now not being the worst is actually pretty good.

Mia You could go to Northampton genuinely, on clearing unis let anyone in that can spell their name.

Aidan And do what?

Mia Just ring them and ask what you could do?

Aidan Medicine, I could be a doctor.

Mia I was thinking more like, business studies, you'd like that, just, anything so you can get the loan really.

Aidan No, I can't because, if I do I'll just ruin it somehow and then be in the same place but with loads of debt, it's a waste of time.

They sit in silence.

Mia No I'm sick of this, show me the trick.

Aidan I can't do it.

Mia No you've been saying that all summer, I'm going away tomorrow, so it's now or never.

Aidan I've never landed it.

Mia Well, you're going to now.

Aidan I'll muck it up.

Mia Maybe.

Aidan Definitely.

Mia Do it.

Aidan It's not going to happen, I'll mess it up, just go away to Bristol and forget about me.

Mia If you get this trick, you have to sign up to the best course you can get into with your college course solely for the student loan and for something to do, and then you'll apply to some new jobs in cafés or wherever won't check a reference properly, and you'll tell your mum you will help out with rent from the loan. You'll meet a nice geeky girl our age and you'll talk about that Japanese video game and stuff you actually like, and you'll come to the pub over Christmas with all my boys' school friends and you'll proudly say that you chose to stay here and you are excited for the future, and you'll come up with legal business ideas, and most of them will fail but you'll learn something from every failure and you'll keep picking yourself up from them because that's all you can do, you'll find the thing that you love and you'll keep doing it until you become good enough at it that someone will give you money. Because I'm sorry but you can't lie on the sofa with your mum, you can't hang out in El Davo's caravan, you've got to be better, no one will help you, and there are people trying to take advantage of you, so it's just up to you to be better. Because your podcasters are right, most people don't care about you, they've got their own stuff going on, so you have to care about yourself. And eventually, you'll do something you will be proud of.

Aidan And if I don't land it.

Mia You give up.

Aidan Right then.

Aidan *stands up, he gets ready to try the trick. He takes it very seriously.*

Mia Believe in yourself.

Aidan Oooga chaka.

Aidan *tries the trick.*

He fails.

Nah, give me another go.

www.ingramcontent.com/pod-product-compliance
Lightning Source LLC
LaVergne TN
LVHW052338100826
845147LV00020B/1110

* 9 7 8 1 3 5 0 6 4 0 3 4 4 *